THE GIFT IN YOU

STUDY GUIDE

Dr. Caroline Leaf

The Gift in You Study Guide

A companion study guide to the book and teaching,
The Gift in You, by Dr. Caroline Leaf

© Copyright 2010 by Caroline Leaf
Design by: Inprov, Ltd.
Licensed by: Dr. Caroline Leaf
Published by: Inprov, Ltd. with licensing permission from Switch on Your Brain International, LLC

All rights are reserved. No part of this publication may be reproduced, stored in a retrieval system or transmitted in any form or by any means, electronic, mechanical, photocopying, recording or otherwise, without the prior written permission of the copyright owners.

Unless otherwise noted, Scripture is taken from the New King James Version. Copyright © 1982 by Thomas Nelson, Inc. Used by permission. All rights reserved.

Disclaimer: The information and solutions offered in this study guide are intended to serve as guidelines for managing toxic thoughts, emotions and bodies. Please discuss specific symptoms and medical conditions with your doctor.

www.drleaf.com

Table of Contents

Part One: The Gift in You — 7

Introduction — 8
Chapter 1: Uncovering Your Hidden Gift — 10
Chapter 2: You Are Not Your Score — 14
Chapter 3: Unlimited You — 20
Chapter 4: Operating in Your Gift — 26
Chapter 5: The Science of Your Gift — 30

Part Two: Uncovering the Gift in You — 35

Chapter 6: An Overview of Your Gift — 36
Chapter 7: The Seven Pillars of Your Gift — 40
Chapter 8: Maximizing Your Gift — 46
Chapter 9: The Structure of Your Gift — 50
Chapter 10: The Gift Profile — 54
Chapter 11: How to Complete the Gift Profile — 58
Chapter 12: What Your Gift Profile Says about You — 72

Part Three: Choosing to Live Out Your Gift — 77

Introduction — 79
Chapter 13: Love and Fear — 80
Chapter 14: Discomfort Zones — 84
Chapter 15: You *Can* Choose – The Scientific Proof — 88
Chapter 16: You Can Choose the Love Tree or the Fear Tree — 92

Table of Contents Continued

Part Four: Overcoming Gift-Blockers   97
Introduction   99
Chapter 17: Toxic Thoughts as Gift-Blockers   100
Chapter 18: Toxic Emotions as Gift-Blockers   104
Chapter 19: Toxic Words as Gift-Blockers   108
Chapter 20: Toxic Love as a Gift-Blocker   112
Chapter 21: Toxic Dreams as Gift-Blockers   116
Chapter 22: Toxic Choices as Gift-Blockers   120
Chapter 23: Toxic Touch as a Gift-Blocker   124
Chapter 24: Toxic Seriousness as a Gift Blocker   128
Chapter 25: Toxic Seeds of Unforgiveness as Gift-Blockers   132
Conclusion   136

PART ONE:
The Gift in You

Introduction

Maybe no one ever told you that you have a gift. Maybe you've been told but haven't really been able to believe it. Perhaps you discovered your gift but you haven't been living in it or developed it to the greatest potential.

You can discover what your gift is and, by learning its structure, begin to thrive in it.

Over twenty years ago, when I first started researching the science of thought, I could not have predicted that the science of neurons, dendrites and cells could help unlock potential, gifting and freedom. That's why I'm so passionate about the science of thought – it helps us to understand our gift and how to use it. All day long we are thinking. We even think at night to sort out our ideas while we are sleeping!

God has given us this ability to think and make decisions based on how we think, and each of us does this in our own unique way: this is our gift. This wonderful gift will manifest in many different ways in what we say and do.

What is your gift – the special way that you think? Do you believe what you have inside of you is unique to you, completely different from anyone else?

Understanding how our gift is structured is just the beginning, but once we start the process, we launch into a lifetime of sharing. You can live in your purpose if you operate in your gift. Understanding how your brain is "wired" will help you understand your thinking and help you use this gift of thinking in your own unique way to its fullest potential.

This study guide is a companion to my book, *The Gift in You,* and is sectioned in four parts. Part One explains the gift in you; Part Two uncovers the gift in you; Part Three shows how to live out your gift; and Part Four shows how to overcome gift-blockers.

Each chapter in the study guide corresponds to a chapter in the book and offers a summary or recap of the book chapter. Key questions for group discussion or personal reflection are included in the summary section. At the end of each chapter, I present a Bible verse for memorization.

Throughout this study guide, I have provided space for you to answer questions and take notes. Some of these questions will provoke deep thinking and therefore require more writing. I encourage you to use the "Notes" section at the end of the chapters to further explore your thoughts and feelings. But I also want you to use this format as a learning tool – or homework, if you will – so you can understand how your brain works, how you think, and how you can maximize your gift.

Are you ready to find out more about your gift, the unique and special way you think?

Let's begin.

> *"I knew you before I formed you in your mother's womb"* (Jeremiah 1:5 NLT).

CHAPTER 1:
UNCOVERING YOUR HIDDEN GIFT

Because we all crave acceptance, sometimes we compare our gift to others' in an attempt to measure if we belong. If you try to adopt an accomplished person's roadmap to success as your own, you will limit yourself and where your gift can take you. You undermine your gift by trying to copy someone else's.

Your spirit and your actions must line up. Neurologically, your brain is wired to function according to a specific sequence, your unique sequence.

Success isn't defined by a collection of assets or an accumulation of power and money. Success is living out God's purpose for your life – using the gifting He has given you. Each of us will express his or her gift differently because every single one of us can do something someone else can't.

Your unique gift, life experiences, the lessons you've learned, all combine to open doors of unlimited potential!

QUESTIONS:

If you have ever compared yourself to others, please explain in detail how you felt after making the comparisons?

_____
_____
_____

Do you really believe what you think and choose to say? In other words, are your thoughts aligned with your word and actions?

_____
_____
_____

CHAPTER 1 Uncovering Your Hidden Gift

Success isn't defined by a collection of assets or an accumulation of power and money. How do you define success?

_____
_____
_____

In my book, *The Gift in You*, how do I define success?

_____
_____
_____

In a training session I once conducted, a teacher adamantly claimed that a child in his class had no gift. Another teacher, who embraced my teaching about the importance of living in our gifting, countered, "That child – that so-called stupid child – can do something you can't do."

Each person can do something no one else can do because of the unique way in which each of us thinks. Do you believe that God has provided this unique gift in you and that no one else thinks quite like you do?

_____
_____
_____

Please explain/describe in detail how you see your gift (how you uniquely think)? How does your unique way of thinking manifest?

_____
_____
_____
_____

THE GIFT IN YOU STUDY GUIDE

MEMORY VERSE

*This is why I remind you to fan into flames the spiritual **gift** God gave you . . .*
(2 Timothy 1:6 NLT).

Write down what this verse means to you.

_____
_____
_____
_____
_____
_____
_____
_____

NOTES

_____
_____
_____
_____
_____
_____
_____
_____
_____
_____

CHAPTER 1 Uncovering Your Hidden Gift

NOTES

> ... be transformed by the renewing of your mind ... (Romans 12:2).

CHAPTER 2
YOU ARE NOT YOUR SCORE

We are designed to seek definition and order in chaos. Electrical impulses pour into our brains from each of our five senses (sight, touch, taste, sound and smell). Our brains have a very sophisticated system to make sense of this flood of incoming information.

In the same way, in life, we seek to label and define each other, but there's no single test that can define an entire being. The slice of information measured in a test is very small compared to the entirety of who we are and who God created us to be.

God is eternity and infinity, and He gifted each of us with a unique piece of His thinking to achieve a unique purpose He designed us to fulfill. We have truth-value.

When we are grouped into boxes – learning disabled, gifted, right-brained, left-brained, overachiever, underachiever – that definition becomes a part of how we see ourselves.

IQ tests and other labels, many times taken at a fairly young age, can follow us the rest of our lives. Today, we can now clearly prove intelligence is not fixed but rather grows and develops with us as we use it – just like our gift.

QUESTIONS:

If you have ever experienced someone placing a label on you because of your intelligence or your skills, please explain how it made you feel.

_____

_____

Do you or did you agree with the label that was placed on you?

_____

CHAPTER 2 You Are Not Your Score

_____

_____

Have you ever labeled others? A spouse, a child, a sibling, a co-worker, a student, etc.? Why?

_____

_____

_____

Do you know if this label impacted the person in a negative or positive way?

_____

_____

_____

Intelligence is not fixed, but rather _____ and _____ with us as we _____ it.

Remember, there is no expiration date on potential!

Renewing our minds is a physical reality and scientific fact. If the brain gets damaged, it can change to compensate. It can rewire itself, which fits in with what God said in Romans 12:2 . . . *be transformed by the renewing of your mind* . . . If we work on how our brains are wired, we can develop and change areas of our brains and live out our true selves.

With the advances in brain imaging techniques, we now have a better view of the brain operating in real time. Brain imaging captures the blood flow supplying oxygen and glucose to hardworking neurons. The more activity in the brain, the more blood will flow to that area.

We now know that the brain never wears out, instead getting better with use. The brain also changes in structure and function throughout our lives. We literally shape our own brains according to the choices we make. I call this the I-factor; scientifically it is known as the science of Epigenetics. Our life experiences also shape our brains.

QUESTIONS:

How can we develop and change areas of our brains?

_____

_____

_____

The more activity in the brain, the more _____ _____ _____ _____ _____.

What is the reshaping of the brain according to the choices we make called?

_____

_____

_____

What else helps reshape our brains?

_____

_____

_____

The diversity in the internal networking of our thoughts (memories), organization and function impacts the way we think and approach life.

Sometimes, what is diagnosed as a learning disability is actually caused by the classroom. Some children are not wired to sit still and absorb information. When we don't work with the structure of our gifting, we can't process information and build memory. For example, a child with a kinesthetic gift structure will learn better sitting on a ball with a side-to-side motion rather than a stationary chair. The motion allows information to enter the brain in sequence with the child's brain wiring.

How you operate, learn and process and what you do with your gift are going to be different for you than for anyone else. Understanding how your brain is wired can unlock your "true-you."

CHAPTER 2 You Are Not Your Score

Your gift helps you celebrate your difference. Don't minimize or squash it so you can look just like everyone else around you. In our differences, we find greatness to glorify our Creator.

QUESTIONS:

What impacts the way we think and approach life?

_____
_____
_____

What can block our ability to process information and build memory?

_____
_____
_____

Children learn differently from each other. As a child, did you ever feel like you were forced to conform in the classroom? If so, how did it make you feel?

_____
_____
_____

What does our gift help us celebrate?

_____
_____
_____
_____

THE GIFT IN YOU STUDY GUIDE

MEMORY VERSE

I praise you because I am fearfully and wonderfully made . . . (Psalm 139:14 NIV).

Write down what this verse means to you.

> "Your gift is the foundation of greatness; using your gift builds genius."
> Dr. Caroline Leaf

_____

_____

_____

_____

_____

_____

_____

_____

NOTES

_____

_____

_____

_____

_____

_____

_____

_____

_____

_____

_____

CHAPTER 2 You Are Not Your Score

NOTES

> ... you knit me together in my mother's womb. I praise you because I am fearfully and wonderfully made ... (Psalm 139:13-14 NIV).

CHAPTER 3
UNLIMITED YOU

You were created intentionally. God knit you together in a particular way, and He did not design you to be limited.

When I first started to study how we think and the uniqueness in the way each of us thinks (our gift), and how the brain processes, the science of thought, I was amazed how giants in the field of neuroscience prove God's Word in their scientific principles.

For years, conventional wisdom said that the brain doesn't grow or change after early childhood; that as we age our brain progressively degenerates; and that once the brain was damaged, it remains that way.

However, the science of neuroplasticity shows the brain has the ability to reorganize itself, changing and altering its structure as we think. The brain can adjust to trauma and rewire toxic thoughts and learning patterns, breaking chains of the past. I saw this in my own research with people suffering from head injury. Neuroplasticity research is outlining the boundless potential of the human brain and providing hope.

Questions:

In a simple definition, how would you define the field of neuroscience?

_____

_____

_____

How do giants in the field of neuroscience prove God's Word?

_____

_____

CHAPTER 3 Unlimited You

Name three (3) items of "conventional wisdom" or old beliefs about the brain.

1. _____
2. _____
3. _____

New science says that the brain can _____ itself and can adjust to _____ and rewire _____ _____ and _____ _____ _____.

Neuroplasticity research is providing hope. What we choose to think about and how we choose to think can switch our genes on and off, changing the structure and function of the brain.

The more we think according to our gift, the more intelligent we can become. The more intelligent we become, the more our gift grows. We quite literally determine our own potential.

Scientists have found that we are 'wired for love,' which means we are designed to build positive and not negative thoughts. This means we learn fear. We can alter brain anatomy in a positive love direction or a negative fear direction by how we think and what we think about, the choices we make and the words we speak. If we build fear pathways with toxic thinking, bitterness, worry, anxiety, anger or unforgiveness, we can wire negative behavior into the brain, potentially creating "gift-blockers." We make this choice.

The plasticity of the brain makes it creative and susceptible to gift-blockers. Scientists call this "plastic paradox," meaning this amazing characteristic used for the wrong purpose can harm rather than heal. Positive change in one area of the brain will lead to positive change in other areas as well. Gift-blockers cause chemical and physical damage to the brain.

Questions:

What we think about and how we think can switch our _____ on and off and change our brain's _____ and _____.

THE GIFT IN YOU STUDY GUIDE

PAGE 22

Name the two directions our brain anatomy can follow.

1. _____

2. _____

Toxic thinking can include bitterness, worry and anxiety. Can you name other toxic thoughts and explain why they can be harmful?

1. _____

2. _____

3. _____

What do scientists call the misuse of the brain's amazing characteristic, plasticity, to harm rather than heal?

_____

_____

_____

What toxic thinking have you experienced?

_____

_____

_____

How did these thought patterns affect your gift, and the resultant talents or skills, which are the manifestations of your gift?

_____

_____

_____

This spiritual principle is key to the release of your truth-value, your unique way of thinking, your gift: If you use what God has given you, you will grow into who He created you to be.

The enemy will use any gift-blocker possible to disorganize your thought life and disconnect you from the Savior. We are called to be good stewards of our minds, our bodies, our potential and our gift. When you surrender to God, one of the many blessings released is your gift. Your gift directs who you are because "as a man thinketh in his heart, so is he."

Because each of us has this unique gift, this amazingly unique and special designer way of thinking, we each walk in our gifting differently. When you walk in your own gift a few things will follow; love is one, intelligence and wisdom are others.

Questions:

What spiritual principle is key to releasing your gift?

_____

_____

_____

List the four items of which we are called to be good stewards:

1. _____
2. _____
3. _____
4. _____

Can you name other things God has placed in our lives and over which He has given us responsibility?

_____

_____

_____

_____

Do you believe you have been a good steward of your gift from God?

_____
_____
_____

When you walk in your own gift, name two things that will follow.

1. _____
2. _____

Memory Verse

But whoever did want him, who believed he was who he claimed and would do what he said, He made to be their true selves, their child-of-God selves (John 1:9 The Message).

Write down what this verse means to you.

> "I want to know God's thoughts . . . the rest are details." Albert Einstein

_____
_____
_____
_____
_____
_____
_____

NOTES

_____
_____
_____

CHAPTER 3 Unlimited You

PAGE 25

NOTES

> "Before you were born I set you apart . . ." (Jeremiah 1:5 NLT).

CHAPTER 4
OPERATING IN YOUR GIFT

Operating in your gift allows you to choose love over fear. When you are at peace and know who you are in Christ, God can use you to help others find where they fit in the puzzle. When we operate in fear of rejection, pain and abuse, we will not believe we are loved and accepted.

God created us as thinking beings, and the science of thought demonstrates this fact. You were designed and created with love and in love to express love. As you think according to your unique way – your gift – love flows and you operate at a higher level.

When you operate in your gift, you operate in wisdom. Read Proverbs 9:1-6; it compares wisdom to building a house on seven columns, preparing a banquet, taking part in the banquet and using the house. This means wisdom and good judgment are built and take time to develop. God's Word consistently says we are to get wisdom. We need to build a house of wisdom in our minds. We need to think clearly according to our gifts to do this.

The brain is also built on Seven Pillars of thought or seven main areas that represent the seven types of thought that make up our gift, which have been revealed through imaging techniques. As people perform different tasks, imaging reveals brain activity.

The adage, "Use it or lose it," is true. The more you think, the more your brain grows, making you wiser.

Questions:

If you're operating in your gift, explain how; if not, explain why not.

_____

_____

CHAPTER 4 Operating in Your Gift

Do you operate in fear of rejection, pain and abuse or do you operate in peace and wisdom?
_____
_____
_____

Name two items which are built and take time to develop.

1. _____
2. _____

What kind of house do we need to build in our minds?
_____
_____
_____

Imaging techniques have revealed brain activity as people do what?
_____
_____
_____

The more you think, what happens to your brain?
_____
_____
_____

What has been your past experience with the science of thought?
_____
_____
_____

Do you believe that the development of your brain is under your own control? Why or why not?

_____

_____

_____

Memory Verse

Wisdom has built her house, She has hewn out her seven pillars (Proverbs 9:1).

Write down what this verse means to you.

_____

_____

_____

_____

NOTES

_____

_____

_____

_____

_____

_____

_____

_____

_____

CHAPTER 4 Operating in Your Gift

NOTES

> *My frame was not hidden from you when I was made in the secret place. When I was woven together . . .* (Psalm 139:15 NIV).

CHAPTER 5
THE SCIENCE OF YOUR GIFT

Your brain is made of around a hundred billion nerve cells, each one looking like a tree with a central cell body and branches. All your memories, which are the same thing as your thoughts, are stored on these nerve cells.

On the left side of the brain, we process from the details to the big picture; on the right side of the brain, we process from the big picture to the details. The two sides of the brain need to be in continual communication. This can only be achieved through thinking. The more we think according to our gift, the more the two sides communicate and the more healthy our brains become. This leads to more branches growing on these nerve cells, increasing their communication with each other and increasing our intelligence. Our brains are designed for deep thought.

When you operate in your gifting, these branches form easily because your brain is working the way it was wired to support your gift.

Albert Einstein harnessed the ability of his gift, developed his gifting and worked with how his brain was wired to achieve what he did. Just like Einstein, each of us can do something no one else can. Understanding the structure of our gift allows us to discover and achieve our purpose.

Questions:

Your brain is made of a hundred billion nerve cells that look like a what?

_____

_____

_____

CHAPTER 5 The Science of Your Gift

PAGE 31

The two sides of the brain must communicate. How do they do this?

_____

What does the left side of the brain allow us to do?

_____

What does the right side of the brain allow us to do?

_____

_____

_____

The more branches that grow on these nerve cells, the more they _____ with each other and the more _____ you become.

Read the information titled, "Einstein's Brain." We can discern from the research on Albert Einstein's brain that as we use our gift, physical change occurs which will be apparent on a _____ and _____ level in the brain.

Einstein's Brain

Following Einstein's death in 1955, the doctor who performed Einstein's autopsy, sectioned and preserved his brain. Interesting discoveries were made over the years. Einstein's brain had a higher ratio of glial cells to neural cells. The theory says that the more glial cells in the brain, the more thinking activity that has occurred. Einstein apparently had more glial cells in the left parietal cortex, the top sides of the brain that process sensory information, spatial orientation, logic, math ability, spatial reasoning and three-dimensional visualization. In 1996, it was discovered that Einstein had a larger parietal lobe and the neurons were packed closely together making communication faster than normal. This probably contributed to Einstein's quick and extremely integrated thinking.

With the understanding of the science of gifting, these areas of his brain were so developed because they were the areas of his gifting, areas which he had developed with his work and discoveries.

Although he did not take the Gift Profile, Einstein, I believe, thought hard and deeply according to his gift. We can glean from this research that as we use our gifts, physical change occurs which will be apparent on a structural and chemical level in the brain.

Read more about Albert Einstein in *The Gift in You*, pages 32-35.

Memory Verse

Wise men store up knowledge. . . (Proverbs 10:14 NIV).

Write down what this verse means to you.

_____
_____
_____

NOTES

NOTES

PART TWO:
Uncovering the Gift in You

> *Wisdom has built her house; she has hewn out its seven pillars* (Proverbs 9:1).

CHAPTER 6
AN OVERVIEW OF YOUR GIFT

Understanding the structure of your gift will help you learn how to maximize it, how you can work to achieve lasting results in any environment, and how you can better relate to others who have their own unique gifts.

We have been taught that each section of the brain is responsible for specific functions, but the brain is sophisticated beyond measure. From modern technological advances, we find that the brain has seven main areas like columns or pillars. According to Scriptures, a house of wisdom is built on Seven Pillars; and according to science, the structure of your gift is built on Seven Pillars of thought.

Your brain's thought trees group together forming Seven Pillars of thought running from the top to the bottom of the brain and across the left and right sides. Each one is responsible for a specific behavioral function and thought. You are a mixture of the seven types of thought which influence how you perceive the world.

Your thoughts (memories) and emotions are stored in the nonconscious part of your mind and influence your conscious thoughts. Toxic thoughts in the nonconscious spill over to the conscious.

The Seven Pillars of Thought:

- Intrapersonal pillar deals with decision-making, planning, analyzing, realizing goals and developing strategies.

- Interpersonal pillar involves social interaction, communication, tuning into others' needs.

- Linguistic pillar deals with the spoken and written language.

CHAPTER 6 An Overview of Your Gift

PAGE 37

- Logical/Mathematical pillar is associated with reasoning, logic, scientific thinking, numbers and problem solving.

- Kinesthetic pillar provides sensory and body awareness.

- Musical pillar is music-based but also includes the "gut instincts."

- Visual/Spatial pillar at the back of the brain imagines and forms mental maps.

Questions:

Understanding your gift structure will help you do three things. What are they?

1. _____

2. _____

3. _____

Your brain's thought trees group together to form Seven Pillars that run from where to where and each are responsible for what?

_____

_____

_____

Where are your thoughts (memories) and emotions stored?

_____

_____

_____

Toxic thoughts in the nonconscious can spill over to the _____ .

As you operate in your gift, in other words, as you are thinking in your special way, each thought loops through the Seven Pillars of thought to trigger memories, thoughts and actions. Each time you think, your brain changes positively. As you work out your gift and use your gift to discover your true self, you will develop your soul and spirit. After all, the Bible says, *Beloved, I pray that you may prosper in all things and be in health, just as your soul prospers* (3 John 1:2).

Name the Seven Pillars of the mind (of thought) and the functions with which these areas deal:

1. _____
2. _____
3. _____
4. _____
5. _____
6. _____
7. _____

As you operate in your gift, each thought loops through the Seven Pillars of thought to trigger_____ and _____.

Memory Verse

Beloved, I pray that you may prosper in all things and be in health, just as your soul prospers (3 John 1:2).

Write down what this verse means to you.

_____
_____
_____
_____
_____
_____

CHAPTER 6 An Overview of Your Gift

NOTES

> *"Let all who are simple come in here,"* she [wisdom] *says to those who lack judgment* (Proverbs 9:4 NIV).

CHAPTER 7
THE SEVEN PILLARS OF YOUR GIFT

We do not all have the same gift, which means each of us thinks differently. This is the concept of the gift. How are they different for each person? The Seven Pillars of thought are interconnected, each responsible for primary functions and particular characteristics. Each person uses all seven of these pillars but differently. This accounts for our uniqueness.

So when you describe yourself, you are always a mixture of all seven types of thought. The way you cycle through the Seven Pillars of thought describes how you are thinking to build the thought. At each pillar the thought is going through a different level of processing. The first pillar of thought tells you how you receive information and acts as the doorway into your mind. Your first pillar could be any one of the seven described in the previous chapter.

So for example, if Intrapersonal thinking is near the top of your thinking pattern, you receive information (because this is what the first pillar does) by being:

- introspective and aware of your range of emotions.
- controlling and working with your thoughts and emotions.
- expressing your thoughts.
- motivated to identify and pursue goals.

Can you name other skills that fall within Intrapersonal thinking?

_____

_____

_____

The Intrapersonal pillar is fundamental to introspection, self-knowledge and understanding your own feelings, thoughts and intuitions.

CHAPTER 7 The Seven Pillars of Your Gift

Do you believe that this best describes the way you start your thinking process? Why or why not?

_____
_____
_____

Remember, any one of the Seven Pillars of thought could be your first one, so you may have for example, Interpersonal thinking near the top of your thinking pattern, which means you receive information (because this is what the first pillar does) by being someone who is:

- full of questions.
- a strong communicator.
- a strong leader.
- good at networking.
- a clever negotiator.
- a skillful teacher.

The Interpersonal thinking area contains the nerve cells responsible for communicating – not simply talking but communicating. Social interaction, listening, sharing, building relationships, giving and receiving love are all primary functions of this pillar of thought.

Can you name other skills that fall within Interpersonal thinking?

_____
_____
_____

If the Linguistic pillar is one of the first steps in the sequence of your gift, you may exhibit these characteristics as you receive information:

- You need to express and explain yourself by writing and/or using lots of words.
- You like to argue, persuade, entertain and instruct.
- You like to write, play with words, read and tell stories.
- You have a good general knowledge.

Can you name other skills that fall within Linguistic thinking?

_____

_____

_____

The Logical/Mathematical pillar of thought deals with scientific reasoning, logic and analysis. This pillar includes the ability to mentally calculate and process logical problems and equations and handle long chains of reasoning in a precise manner.

If the Logical/Mathematical pillar is one of the first steps in the sequence of your gift, you may exhibit these characteristics as you receive information:

- You are intuitive and disciplined in your thinking.
- You like to calculate and quantify.
- You want to reason things out.
- You want to know what's coming up next.

Can you name other skills that fall within Logical/Mathematical thinking?

_____

_____

_____

Kinesthetic thinking is the intelligence of movement and somatic sensation. Your Kinesthetic pillar, the multisensory type of thinking, helps you play soccer or run around, maneuver or experience as you learn, and you build memory through movement.

If the Kinesthetic pillar is one of the first steps in the sequence of your gift, you may exhibit these characteristics as you receive information:

- You have good coordination.
- You show a good sense of timing.
- You approach problems physically.
- You explore your environment through touch and movement.

CHAPTER 7 The Seven Pillars of Your Gift

Can you name other skills that fall within Kinesthetic thinking?

_____

_____

_____

In addition to an ability to sing or play a musical instrument, Musical thinking includes the ability to read patterns, identify rhythm and follow instincts. Musical thinkers build memory through rhythm and intuition.

If the Musical pillar is one of the first steps in the sequence of your gift, you may exhibit these characteristics as you receive information:

- You instinctively feel when things are right or wrong.
- You don't do things unless they "feel" right.
- You can't always explain why but you know when someone is to be trusted or not to be trusted.
- You are highly sensitive to your surroundings.

Can you name other skills that fall within Musical thinking?

_____

_____

_____

The Visual/Spatial thinking pillar includes the ability to see color, light, shape and depth and to imagine things. Visual/Spatial thinkers see with the mind and act on initial perceptions. They build memory through abstract language and imagery.

If the Visual/Spatial pillar of thought is one of the first steps in the sequence of your gift, you may exhibit these characteristics as you receive information:

- You often stare off into space while listening.
- You enjoy hands-on activities or learning by seeing and doing.
- You recognize faces but may not remember names.
- You navigate through spaces well. You can easily find your way through traffic.

Can you name other skills that fall within Visual/Spatial thinking?

_____
_____
_____

Memory Verse

Guard the good deposit that was entrusted to you – guard it with the help of the Holy Spirit who lives in us (2 Timothy 1:14 NIV).

Write down what this verse means to you.

_____
_____
_____
_____
_____
_____
_____
_____
_____
_____
_____
_____
_____

CHAPTER 7 The Seven Pillars of Your Gift

NOTES

My people are destroyed for lack of knowledge (Hosea 4:6).

CHAPTER 8
MAXIMIZING YOUR GIFT

Understanding the structure of your gift is imperative to living out your gifting because you will understand better who you are. When we determine the structure of your gift — the order of the pillars of thought that your brain uses to process information according to the proper sequence — we can determine triggers to maximize your brain function during every step. You can also catch yourself when you step out of your gifting and into gift-blocking which will harm you and not heal you.

In the Gift Profile, how high your score is for each of the pillars determines how profound that trait is in your gift and your personality, but all seven describe you, not just the top score. So you can't call yourself a Kinesthetic learner or Intrapersonal learner; you are a mixture of all seven. So the order of the scores on the Gift Profile describes you — and you are your own category.

Thoughts loop through your Seven Pillars of thought, and each loop contributes to a deeper understanding of the information. This is a bit like digestion of food: as you cycle through your unique order of the Seven Pillars of thought (determined by the profile), you are digesting the information to build a physical thought in your brain.

Questions:

In your own words, describe how I have defined the structure of your gift.

_____

_____

_____

_____

CHAPTER 8 Maximizing Your Gift

What are the seven steps that our thoughts must complete to develop, process and complete thoughts? (See *The Gift in You*, page 79.)

_____

_____

_____

Do you understand what your unique gift is? If so, please explain.

_____

_____

_____

The gift concept helps us see each other through Jesus' eyes. Read pages 72-76 of *The Gift in You*, where I explain the structure of my children's gifts. List my children's gift combinations below, then name someone who shares similar gift structures. A very important note here: someone may seem similar on the surface but when you compare their similarities, there will be more differences than similarities. We are all completely unique in our gift. So once you have named someone who is similar, describe him or her more fully and you will see the differences.

Jessica:

Do you know someone who shares similar gift structures?
Describe their differences.

_____

_____

Dominique:

Do you know someone who shares similar gift structures?
Describe their differences.

_____

_____

Jeffrey:

Do you know someone who shares similar gift structures? Describe their differences.

_____
_____
_____

Alexandria:

Do you know someone who shares similar gift structures? Describe their differences.

_____
_____
_____

Memory Verse

Wisdom, like an inheritance, is a good thing . . . (Ecclesiastes 7:11 NIV).

Write down what this verse means to you.

_____
_____
_____
_____

> "You don't have to be like Einstein to be intelligent; you just need to find your gift so you can reach your full potential." Dr. Caroline Leaf

CHAPTER 8 Maximizing Your Gift

NOTES

> ... he has given each one of us a special gift through the generosity of Christ (Ephesians 4:7 NLT).

CHAPTER 9
THE STRUCTURE OF YOUR GIFT

Your brain is made up of approximately 100 billion neurons that can potentially connect 100 trillion times or more. These neurons are clustered into Seven Pillars or columns of thinking that stretch from the top to the bottom and left to right across the brain. Your brain has an incredible infinite capacity for thought and intelligence.

As I have been sharing with you, individuality and giftedness come from the different arrangements of the pillars of thinking. If the arrangement of your pillars indicates that linguistics is the first pillar activated in your thought structure, as neurons fire in your temporal lobe, where language is processed, the firing neurons will be amplified to reflect a higher level of skill. You would be eloquent with words. But this linguistic pillar would not work alone, it would work hand-in-hand with the other six pillars to describe your gift. Remember, however, that **all** combinations are good.

Use the wonderful feelings you get when you understand something, as a guide that you are using your gift. The converse applies: you will feel a lack of peace and fuzzy thinking when your gift is blocked.

The deeper and harder you think, the greater the interaction between your Seven Pillars of thought and the greater your wisdom.

God formed you a certain way, but it's up to you to use what He has given you. Your gift has purpose. Your gift is intentional.

Questions:

Where are the neurons clustered?

_____

CHAPTER 9 The Structure of Your Gift

From where do individuality and giftedness originate?

_____
_____
_____

What is the meaning of the statement: "Your gift has purpose and is intentional?"

_____
_____
_____

Memory Verse

This is why I remind you to fan into flames the spiritual gift God gave you when I laid my hands on you (2 Timothy 1:6 NLT).

Write down what this verse means to you.

_____

_____

> "Your gift will inspire you to go beyond yourself." Dr. Caroline Leaf

_____
_____
_____
_____
_____
_____

NOTES

CHAPTER 9 The Structure of Your Gift

NOTES

> ... for I am fearfully and wonderfully made (Psalm 139:14).

CHAPTER 10
THE GIFT PROFILE

The Gift Profile is not a diagnostic test but a discovery of your gift structure to help you maximize your gift and uncover the "true you." We think according to our gift. The more we think, the more our brains grow. Self-regulating our thinking helps build our gift, intelligence and wisdom.

The Gift Profile reassures us that when we continually use our gift, we enhance and preserve our brains' powers as we live our daily lives. Once you have completed and scored the profile, you will find the order of your unique process of thinking — the description of your gift.

Your thought process (your gift) is the interaction of a combination of all Seven Pillars of thought. We do not have weakness in our design because we are made in God's image; we learn weakness through incorrect thinking or thinking out of our gifting. God has designed our brains in such a way that we can overcome our weaknesses using our strengths. To live in your gift, to achieve you divine sense of purpose, you must know how your brain is wired.

Questions:

We think according to our _____, and the more we think, the more our _____ _____.

What happens when we continually use our gift?
_____
_____
_____
_____

CHAPTER 10 The Gift Profile

What do you like doing best?

_____
_____
_____

What kind of activities appeal to you?

_____
_____
_____

What do you consider your best skills?

_____
_____
_____

Now, it's time to work out your Gift Profile.

> Rabbit went to school and was so excited that he signed up for all the classes, including swimming lessons. As the school term started, Rabbit was full of passion and enthusiasm. His grades in hopping, running and jumping were great, but his swimming was terrible. He got terrible grades in that class. The teacher told Rabbit to stop running, hopping and jumping lessons and just concentrate on swimming. Well, you can guess what happened to Rabbit. He drowned.
>
> This simple yet powerful analogy reflects what's happening when the drive to improve our weaknesses overshadows our strengths.

THE GIFT IN YOU STUDY GUIDE

Memory Verse

In his grace, God has given us different gifts for doing certain things well . . . (Romans 12:6 NLT).

Write down what this verse means to you.

_____

_____

_____

NOTES

_____

_____

_____

_____

_____

_____

_____

_____

_____

_____

_____

_____

_____

_____

CHAPTER 10 The Gift Profile

NOTES

For God's gifts and his call can never be withdrawn (Romans 11:29 NLT).

CHAPTER 11
HOW TO COMPLETE THE GIFT PROFILE

The Gift Profile was developed to help you understand the science of thought and to evaluate the structure of your gifting. We all have a gift; the unique way in which we think which is different from everyone else. This profile is designed to help find this unique way you build thoughts and to encourage and guide us in strengthening both our strong and weak areas.

You can complete the profile by circling "yes" or "no" to the questions in each of the seven categories of intelligences, each representing one of the Seven Pillars of thought making up your gift. Go with your gut instinct and first reaction when answering each question to get the most accurate results, answering yes to the things you enjoy and no to the things you don't. The good news is that there *is no wrong answer!*

If you have several traits you have become good at or skills that you have acquired through life experiences, having learned them through work or school, you may need to complete the profile twice, once for work and your developed skills and once for personal use and fun and your natural skills. Remember: There is no wrong answer.

The Gift Profile Questionnaire

Intrapersonal Thinking

(Please answer questions 1-30 on pages 100-102 in *The Gift in You*.)

	PERSONAL	PROFESSIONAL/ACADEMIC
1.	YES NO	YES NO
2.	YES NO	YES NO

CHAPTER 11 How to Complete the Gift Profile

PAGE 59

	PERSONAL		**PROFESSIONAL/ACADEMIC**	
3.	YES	NO	YES	NO
4.	YES	NO	YES	NO
5.	YES	NO	YES	NO
6.	YES	NO	YES	NO
7.	YES	NO	YES	NO
8.	YES	NO	YES	NO
9.	YES	NO	YES	NO
10.	YES	NO	YES	NO
11.	YES	NO	YES	NO
12.	YES	NO	YES	NO
13.	YES	NO	YES	NO
14.	YES	NO	YES	NO
15.	YES	NO	YES	NO
16.	YES	NO	YES	NO
17.	YES	NO	YES	NO
18.	YES	NO	YES	NO
19.	YES	NO	YES	NO
20.	YES	NO	YES	NO
21.	YES	NO	YES	NO
22.	YES	NO	YES	NO
23.	YES	NO	YES	NO
24.	YES	NO	YES	NO
25.	YES	NO	YES	NO
26.	YES	NO	YES	NO

	PERSONAL		PROFESSIONAL/ACADEMIC	
27.	YES	NO	YES	NO
28.	YES	NO	YES	NO
29.	YES	NO	YES	NO
30.	YES	NO	YES	NO

Interpersonal Thinking
(Please answer questions 1-30 on pages 102-104 in *The Gift in You*.)

	PERSONAL		PROFESSIONAL/ACADEMIC	
1.	YES	NO	YES	NO
2.	YES	NO	YES	NO
3.	YES	NO	YES	NO
4.	YES	NO	YES	NO
5.	YES	NO	YES	NO
6.	YES	NO	YES	NO
7.	YES	NO	YES	NO
8.	YES	NO	YES	NO
9.	YES	NO	YES	NO
10.	YES	NO	YES	NO
11.	YES	NO	YES	NO
12.	YES	NO	YES	NO
13.	YES	NO	YES	NO
14.	YES	NO	YES	NO
15.	YES	NO	YES	NO
16.	YES	NO	YES	NO
17.	YES	NO	YES	NO

CHAPTER 11 How to Complete the Gift Profile

	PERSONAL		PROFESSIONAL/ACADEMIC	
18.	YES	NO	YES	NO
19.	YES	NO	YES	NO
20.	YES	NO	YES	NO
21.	YES	NO	YES	NO
22.	YES	NO	YES	NO
23.	YES	NO	YES	NO
24.	YES	NO	YES	NO
25.	YES	NO	YES	NO
26.	YES	NO	YES	NO
27.	YES	NO	YES	NO
28.	YES	NO	YES	NO
29.	YES	NO	YES	NO
30.	YES	NO	YES	NO

Linguistic Thinking
(Please answer questions 1-30 on pages 105-107 in *The Gift in You*.)

	PERSONAL		PROFESSIONAL/ACADEMIC	
1.	YES	NO	YES	NO
2.	YES	NO	YES	NO
3.	YES	NO	YES	NO
4.	YES	NO	YES	NO
5.	YES	NO	YES	NO
6.	YES	NO	YES	NO
7.	YES	NO	YES	NO
8.	YES	NO	YES	NO

	PERSONAL		PROFESSIONAL/ACADEMIC	
9.	YES	NO	YES	NO
10.	YES	NO	YES	NO
11.	YES	NO	YES	NO
12.	YES	NO	YES	NO
13.	YES	NO	YES	NO
14.	YES	NO	YES	NO
15.	YES	NO	YES	NO
16.	YES	NO	YES	NO
17.	YES	NO	YES	NO
18.	YES	NO	YES	NO
19.	YES	NO	YES	NO
20.	YES	NO	YES	NO
21.	YES	NO	YES	NO
22.	YES	NO	YES	NO
23.	YES	NO	YES	NO
24.	YES	NO	YES	NO
25.	YES	NO	YES	NO
26.	YES	NO	YES	NO
27.	YES	NO	YES	NO
28.	YES	NO	YES	NO
29.	YES	NO	YES	NO
30.	YES	NO	YES	NO

CHAPTER 11 How to Complete the Gift Profile

Logical/Mathematical Thinking
(Please answer questions 1-30 on pages 107-109 in *The Gift in You*.)

	PERSONAL		PROFESSIONAL/ACADEMIC	
1.	YES	NO	YES	NO
2.	YES	NO	YES	NO
3.	YES	NO	YES	NO
4.	YES	NO	YES	NO
5.	YES	NO	YES	NO
6.	YES	NO	YES	NO
7.	YES	NO	YES	NO
8.	YES	NO	YES	NO
9.	YES	NO	YES	NO
10.	YES	NO	YES	NO
11.	YES	NO	YES	NO
12.	YES	NO	YES	NO
13.	YES	NO	YES	NO
14.	YES	NO	YES	NO
15.	YES	NO	YES	NO
16.	YES	NO	YES	NO
17.	YES	NO	YES	NO
18.	YES	NO	YES	NO
19.	YES	NO	YES	NO
20.	YES	NO	YES	NO
21.	YES	NO	YES	NO
22.	YES	NO	YES	NO

	PERSONAL		PROFESSIONAL/ACADEMIC	
23.	YES	NO	YES	NO
24.	YES	NO	YES	NO
25.	YES	NO	YES	NO
26.	YES	NO	YES	NO
27.	YES	NO	YES	NO
28.	YES	NO	YES	NO
29.	YES	NO	YES	NO
30.	YES	NO	YES	NO

Kinesthetic Thinking

(Please answer questions 1-30 on pages 109-112 in *The Gift in You*.)

	PERSONAL		PROFESSIONAL/ACADEMIC	
1.	YES	NO	YES	NO
2.	YES	NO	YES	NO
3.	YES	NO	YES	NO
4.	YES	NO	YES	NO
5.	YES	NO	YES	NO
6.	YES	NO	YES	NO
7.	YES	NO	YES	NO
8.	YES	NO	YES	NO
9.	YES	NO	YES	NO
10.	YES	NO	YES	NO
11.	YES	NO	YES	NO
12.	YES	NO	YES	NO
13.	YES	NO	YES	NO

	PERSONAL		PROFESSIONAL/ACADEMIC	
14.	YES	NO	YES	NO
15.	YES	NO	YES	NO
16.	YES	NO	YES	NO
17.	YES	NO	YES	NO
18.	YES	NO	YES	NO
19.	YES	NO	YES	NO
20.	YES	NO	YES	NO
21.	YES	NO	YES	NO
22.	YES	NO	YES	NO
23.	YES	NO	YES	NO
24.	YES	NO	YES	NO
25.	YES	NO	YES	NO
26.	YES	NO	YES	NO
27.	YES	NO	YES	NO
28.	YES	NO	YES	NO
29.	YES	NO	YES	NO
30.	YES	NO	YES	NO

Musical Thinking
(Please answer questions 1-30 on pages 112-114 in *The Gift in You*.)

	PERSONAL		PROFESSIONAL/ACADEMIC	
1.	YES	NO	YES	NO
2.	YES	NO	YES	NO
3.	YES	NO	YES	NO
4.	YES	NO	YES	NO

	PERSONAL		PROFESSIONAL/ACADEMIC	
5.	YES	NO	YES	NO
6.	YES	NO	YES	NO
7.	YES	NO	YES	NO
8.	YES	NO	YES	NO
9.	YES	NO	YES	NO
10.	YES	NO	YES	NO
11.	YES	NO	YES	NO
12.	YES	NO	YES	NO
13.	YES	NO	YES	NO
14.	YES	NO	YES	NO
15.	YES	NO	YES	NO
16.	YES	NO	YES	NO
17.	YES	NO	YES	NO
18.	YES	NO	YES	NO
19.	YES	NO	YES	NO
20.	YES	NO	YES	NO
21.	YES	NO	YES	NO
22.	YES	NO	YES	NO
23.	YES	NO	YES	NO
24.	YES	NO	YES	NO
25.	YES	NO	YES	NO
26.	YES	NO	YES	NO
27.	YES	NO	YES	NO
28.	YES	NO	YES	NO

CHAPTER 11 How to Complete the Gift Profile

	PERSONAL		PROFESSIONAL/ACADEMIC	
29.	YES	NO	YES	NO
30.	YES	NO	YES	NO

Visual/Spatial Thinking
(Please answer questions 1-30 on pages 114-117 in *The Gift in You*.)

	PERSONAL		PROFESSIONAL/ACADEMIC	
1.	YES	NO	YES	NO
2.	YES	NO	YES	NO
3.	YES	NO	YES	NO
4.	YES	NO	YES	NO
5.	YES	NO	YES	NO
6.	YES	NO	YES	NO
7.	YES	NO	YES	NO
8.	YES	NO	YES	NO
9.	YES	NO	YES	NO
10.	YES	NO	YES	NO
11.	YES	NO	YES	NO
12.	YES	NO	YES	NO
13.	YES	NO	YES	NO
14.	YES	NO	YES	NO
15.	YES	NO	YES	NO
16.	YES	NO	YES	NO
17.	YES	NO	YES	NO
18.	YES	NO	YES	NO
19.	YES	NO	YES	NO

	PERSONAL		PROFESSIONAL/ACADEMIC	
20.	YES	NO	YES	NO
21.	YES	NO	YES	NO
22.	YES	NO	YES	NO
23.	YES	NO	YES	NO
24.	YES	NO	YES	NO
25.	YES	NO	YES	NO
26.	YES	NO	YES	NO
27.	YES	NO	YES	NO
28.	YES	NO	YES	NO
29.	YES	NO	YES	NO
30.	YES	NO	YES	NO

When the profile is completed, the order shows you how you cycle through the seven types of thought to make up your gift.

List the order of your Gift Profile:

PERSONAL

1. _____
2. _____
3. _____
4. _____
5. _____
6. _____
7. _____

PROFESSIONAL/ACADEMIC

1. _____
2. _____
3. _____
4. _____
5. _____
6. _____
7. _____

CHAPTER 11 How to Complete the Gift Profile

Questions:

Do you have different skills that come naturally to you and others that you developed by adapting to your surroundings and circumstances? Explain:

_____

_____

_____

How does the order of the profile align with how you see yourself or would describe yourself?

_____

_____

_____

How different was your personal profile from your professional/academic profile?

_____

_____

_____

What skills have you developed to adapt to your life/work environment?

_____

_____

_____

What has the result of the profile revealed to you about your interaction with others?

_____

_____

What has the profile revealed about the ways you react to situations?

_____
_____
_____
_____
_____

Can you see how your gift may have become blocked (your thinking became fuzzy) as you reacted incorrectly to people or situations? Describe these incidents.

_____
_____
_____
_____
_____

Memory Verse

There are different kinds of spiritual gifts, but the same Spirit is the source of them all (1 Corinthians 12:4 NLT).

Write down what this verse means to you.

_____
_____
_____
_____
_____

NOTES

THE GIFT IN YOU STUDY GUIDE

> *It is the one and only Spirit who distributes all these gifts. He alone decides which gift each person should have* (1 Corinthians 12:11NLT).

CHAPTER 12
WHAT YOUR GIFT PROFILE SAYS ABOUT YOU

Fill in your scores from the questionnaire in the table below to create your Gift Profile. Now, add up the total "yes" choices for each of the seven sections. Then put each as a score out of 30. Next, multiply that number by 100 to get your percentage. For example, 15/30 X 100 = 50%.

	THE ORDER OF THE GIFT	1st Profile (Personal)	1st Profile (Professional)
1.	Intrapersonal Intelligence		
2.	Interpersonal Intelligence		
3.	Linguistic Intellingence		
4.	Logical/Mathematical Intelligence		
5.	Kinesthetic Intelligence		
6.	Musical Intelligence		
7.	Visual/Spatial Intelligence		

Example order of someone's gift:
1. Intrapersonal Intelligence
2. Interpersonal Intelligence
3. Linguistic Intelligence
4. Logical/Mathematical Intelligence
5. Musical Intelligence
6. Visual/Spatial Intelligence
7. Kinesthetic

CHAPTER 12 What Your Gift Profile Says about You

Sometimes the way you think best – the way your brain is really wired – may be very different from the way you thought you processed information.

The first step toward harnessing the powers of your intellect is to recognize we are all uniquely made – no one is better than anyone else.

Creativity is expressed through all the Seven Pillars of thought, working together and directed by the top two.

When you live according to your gift, you step into your truth-value, you will grow much more in intelligence and become more likely to live a happy, fulfilled life.

As you work on your Gift Profile, find out which of the pillars of thought is making the most profound impact on you . . . this is normally the top two in your scores. Though your stronger top two types of thinking will dominate your thinking process, the other five non-dominant types of thinking have to work with the two to complete the cycle of digesting and building the thoughts into networks in your brain that you can use intelligently. Therefore you **need** to develop all seven. As you work in your gift, manifestation will happen: you will write a great report, sing a song, complete a work task successfully and so on. So we don't want to confuse the manifestation of the gift (what we do/say/perform, etc.) with the actual gift (how we uniquely think).

If, for example, you have an area of weakness that you would like to strengthen at work or at home, you use your top two to kick start the process of improving, and this action will draw the other five types of thought in.

So, let's say you want to improve your ability to present information concisely, and musical and intrapersonal are your top two pillars. You could play some music quietly and imagine you are inside your own head introspecting while you are presenting.

Now, let's take a look at what might be standing in the way of your greatest potential – your greatest purpose.

Questions:

In what ways is your gift manifesting? Can it be improved?

_____
_____
_____

Are you underachieving? If yes, how has the Gift Profile shown you this?

_____
_____
_____

Describe the manifestation of your gift.

_____
_____
_____

Memory Verse

Be sure to give to the Lord the best portions of the gifts given to you (Numbers 18:29 NLT).

Write down what this verse means to you.

_____
_____
_____
_____

CHAPTER 12 What Your Gift Profile Says about You

"If the human brain were so simple that we could understand it, we would be so simple that we couldn't." Emerson M. Pugh

NOTES

PART THREE:
Choosing to Live Out Your Gift

Introduction

He has made everything beautiful in its time. He also has planted eternity in men's hearts and minds [a divinely implanted sense of a purpose working through the ages which nothing under the sun but God alone can satisfy] . . . (Ecclesiastes 3:11 AMP).

In Part Three, we will explore the structure of your gift to see what may be keeping you from your full potential. Toxic seeds, no matter how small, can grow into gift-blockers. When gift-blockers are in action, attitude – the cluster of thoughts with emotions attached – is affected.

- Attitude cannot be hidden.
- Attitude is the state of your spirit and mind influencing your choices, which in turn influence your words and your behavior.
- Attitude is tangible – we can feel it because of the chemicals released.

We must adopt the guiding principle: **We can't control our life circumstances, but we can choose to control our attitude and our reaction to the circumstances.**

You can walk in the gift God has given you with confidence and purpose.

> There is no fear in love. But perfect love drives out fear, because fear has to do with punishment. The one who fears is not made perfect in love (1 John 4:18 NIV).

CHAPTER 13
LOVE AND FEAR

Every type of emotion has one of only two roots – love or fear. Science has shown us that we are 'wired for love' and that we learn fear: we have the power to choose. Science has also proven that when we are in fear mode, we will get caught in a cycle of chemical and neurological responses that dominate and dictate the choices we make and the reactions we set in motion.

When we operate in fear, our gifting is blocked, our body is sent into stress mode, and we experience a cycle of toxic chemical and neurological responses. Fear fills our nonconscious with toxic thoughts.

Fear is actually a learned trait. Acting in love releases the chemicals oxytocin and dopamine which help rewire the brain with nontoxic thoughts and rebuild memories. Endorphins and serotonin are also released to help us gain the confidence and motivation needed to face our circumstances.

Love is much more powerful than fear, and because our brains were made to operate in love, growing in love can give you an even greater advantage over fear. **When you operate in your gift, the divine piece of eternity God has planted within you, you step into your destiny. You go from great to genius.**

Questions:

Every type of emotion has one of only two roots. What are they?

_____

_____

_____

_____

CHAPTER 13 Love and Fear

What does fear fill our minds with? List all the negative emotions you can think of that grow out of the root of fear.

_____
_____
_____

List all the positive emotions you can think of that grow out of love.

_____
_____
_____

In what parts of your life are you living in fear? Be specific about what type of fear, for example, irritation.

_____
_____
_____

What has caused you to be ruled by fear in these areas?

_____
_____
_____

How have these fears affected your day-to-day life?

_____
_____
_____
_____

Do you have health problems possibly caused by toxic thoughts?

_____
_____
_____

How can you use love to overcome these fears?

_____
_____
_____

How does acting out in love affect your emotions?

_____
_____
_____

What can you do to strengthen love's power over fear in your mind?

_____
_____
_____

Memory Verse

For God has not given us a spirit of fear . . . but of power, love, and self-discipline (2 Timothy 1:7 NLT).

Write down what this verse means to you.

_____
_____

> "Passion inspires genius to grow."
> Dr. Caroline Leaf

_____

CHAPTER 13 Love and Fear

NOTES

> *Now may the Lord of peace himself give you peace at all times and in every way. The Lord be with all of you* (2 Thessalonians 3:16 NIV).

CHAPTER 14
DISCOMFORT ZONES

Discomfort can indicate a potential gift blocker on two different levels – the "just aware" level and the "adrenaline-pumping, heart-pounding" level – and both can be easily felt due to how they impact the body's electrical and chemical reactions. This is God's gracious way of helping us "feel" in our bodies when we are operating out of our gift.

The job of the "just aware" zone guards the mind. When incoming information is negative our thinking is disrupted by a stress-causing chemical released into the brain. However, when incoming information is positive and love-based, our wisdom is increased and we feel at ease. When toxic thoughts get past the "just aware" level, the chemicals that begin flowing will soon cause your attitude to reach the "adrenaline-pumping, heart-pounding" level. When you begin to experience stress that doesn't dissipate with time, it is a sign that one or more gift-blockers have set in.

By training ourselves to identify our discomfort zones, we can prevent discomforts from causing toxic thoughts and becoming gift-blockers. God has given us a way to overcome these gift-blockers with a part of the brain called the frontal cortex, which empowers us to stand outside of ourselves and observe our own thinking. More specifically, the prefrontal cortex (PFC) helps us use reason and understand our thoughts and control our emotions and stress responses. It helps us restore balance to the brain by allowing us to acknowledge toxic thoughts and decide whether to keep living under their power.

Questions:

Define the "just aware" and "adrenaline-pumping, heart-pounding" levels.

_____

_____

CHAPTER 14 Discomfort Zones

What does the part of the brain, called the prefrontal cortex, help us do?

_____
_____
_____

Identify areas in your life where you experience discomfort.

_____
_____
_____

What stressors are causing you to experience discomfort?

_____
_____
_____

What emotions or feelings do you have that can be clues of potential gift-blockers?

_____
_____
_____

How can you take control of these emotions?

_____
_____
_____

How can you alleviate the stress you experience?

_____
_____

What gift-blockers can you identify?

_____
_____
_____

How can you let go of these gift-blockers and escape their control over your emotions?

_____
_____
_____

Memory Verse

No eye has seen, no ear has heard, no mind has conceived what God has prepared for those who love him (1 Corinthians 2:9 NIV).

Write down what this verse means to you.

_____
_____
_____
_____
_____
_____
_____
_____

CHAPTER 14 Discomfort Zones

NOTES

> *May the Lord direct your hearts . . .* (2 Thessalonians 3:5 NIV).

CHAPTER 15
YOU CAN CHOOSE – THE SCIENTIFIC PROOF

The parallels between science and Scripture are remarkable. You **can** renew your mind. You **can** choose whether you would like to grow a healthy "love attitude" tree that brings health and life into your brain or choose a toxic thorny "fear attitude" tree that will bring death to your brain (see "Love Tree and Fear Tree" on pages 144-145, *The Gift in You*).

With God's help you have the ability to make good decisions. You have the ability to override conscious and nonconscious memories – both toxic and nontoxic – and choose how to respond.

Your ability to choose and make decisions occurs in the frontal lobe, the front part of the brain. Information swirls through the middle of the brain in a tube called the hippocampus around an area called the corpus callosum. As information – your thoughts – moves toward the frontal lobe, it becomes amplified and highly active, building expectancy or hope. Neurotransmitters are released, creating a healthy electrical-chemical love environment in which the memory can be built.

This combination of your thoughts and the neurotransmitters activates a switch on the gene, and building blocks – proteins – are released. These proteins are used to build a branch which holds the new piece of memory.

A temporary memory is born, and you must focus on it, memorize it, study it, or it will disappear after about 48 hours. God's design is so magnificent; once the memory has moved from the nonconscious to the conscious, it stabilizes as toxic or nontoxic. So it is our thoughts, and the decisions based on these thoughts, which cause the memory to be non-toxic or toxic. I call this the "I-factor" and this means it is me, myself and I that influence the changes in the brain structure. You can choose whether you would like to grow a healthy "love attitude" tree that brings health and life into your brain or choose a toxic thorny "fear attitude"

CHAPTER 15 You Can Choose – The Scientific Proof

tree that will bring death to your brain. We can change it. We can change our toxic thoughts, our gift-blockers. We can renew our minds!

Questions:

Where does your ability to make decisions occur?

_____
_____
_____

What are neurotransmitters and what do they create?

_____
_____
_____

Describe in your own words the process of building a memory.

_____
_____
_____

Explain how you feel when you finally understand something you've been studying or thinking about.

_____
_____
_____

Do you believe that you can renew your mind?

_____
_____

Memory Verse

. . . I place before you Life and Death, Blessing and Curse. Choose life so that you and your children will live (Deuteronomy 30:19 *The Message*).

Write down what this verse means to you.

_____
_____
_____
_____
_____
_____
_____
_____

NOTES

_____
_____
_____
_____
_____
_____
_____
_____

CHAPTER 15 You Can Choose – The Scientific Proof

NOTES

> . . . *the fruit of the Spirit is love, joy, peace, patience, kindness, goodness, faithfulness, gentleness and self-control* (Galatians 5:22-23).

CHAPTER 16
YOU CAN CHOOSE THE LOVE TREE OR THE FEAR TREE

You have worked through the profile to find and interpret your gift, and I have shown you, from a scientific perspective, that choice is a brain fact. You **can** choose your reactions to life's circumstances.

There are consequences to investing in your thought life in either the fear or love direction. Our thoughts are the roots, and the effects of our thoughts are the branches, fruits and leaves of the tree.

Our gifts – how we think – can select, modify and regulate gene activity. Our genes don't control our thoughts; our thoughts control our genes – this is the "I-factor' I spoke about earlier. Our perceptions of life shape our biology and the character of our lives. Your gift operates best in a peaceful, love-based, not fear-based, environment.

Thoughts are the mind's fuel and directly influence how the brain controls the body, including the brain. If you choose to see a world filled with love, wonder and beauty, your brain and body will respond by growing in health. If you choose to believe in a dark world filled with fear, your brain and body will become toxic and sick.

In the Fear Tree, the twelve roots are the twelve areas of toxic thinking that flourish in fearful soil (see page 145, *The Gift in You*). Around 87–95% of mental and physical illness come from the thought life; these illnesses are the bad fruit on the tree. The Love Tree's roots are healthy and loving thoughts, emotions, words, and other elements that nourish your gift. This tree grows in the soil of love, trust, perseverance, faith, joy, peace, kindness, gentleness, and self-control.

CHAPTER 16 You Can Choose the Love Tree or the Fear Tree

In Part Four of the Study Guide, we will work on how to uproot gift-blockers and start walking in your gift!

Questions:

Our thoughts are the _____ of the tree, and the effects of our thoughts are _____, _____ and _____ of the tree.

Name elements of the Love Tree's roots. (Healthy thinking is one element.)

_____
_____
_____

The Love Tree grows in what kind of soil?

_____
_____
_____

How do you typically react to negative circumstances in your life?

_____
_____
_____

Has your negative thinking ever impacted your health and well-being?

_____
_____
_____
_____

If so, can you describe the situation in which this occurred?

_____

_____

_____

Memory Verse

And the peace of God, which transcends all understanding, will guard your hearts and your minds in Christ Jesus (Philippians 4:7 NIV).

Write down what this verse means to you.

_____

_____

_____

_____

NOTES

_____

_____

_____

_____

_____

_____

_____

_____

_____

CHAPTER 16 You Can Choose the Love Tree or the Fear Tree

NOTES

PART FOUR:
Overcoming Gift-Blockers

Introduction

Each of us has an amazing gift, a unique and special way of thinking, and as we go through life and interact with others, we use and develop our gift. Unfortunately, we have toxic thought clusters that can affect how well we use our gift and how effectively our gift develops.

Toxic seeds can grow into branches and some include:

- Physical manifestations – for example: cardiovascular problems, digestive problems, immune system disorders, skin disorders
- Learning manifestations – for example: learning disorders, underachieving potential
- Anxiety disorders – for example: phobias, obsessive-compulsive disorders, post traumatic stress disorders, panic attacks
- Depressive disorders
- Addictions

There are twelve areas of toxic categories in our lives that form the roots of the "Fear Tree." (See the image of the Fear Tree on page 145 of *The Gift in You*). Toxic thoughts can poison our minds and bodies. These twelve toxic categories are clustered into the following groups which can grow into gift-blockers:

Toxic Thoughts
Toxic Emotions
Toxic Words
Toxic Love/Faith
Toxic Dreams
Toxic Choices
Toxic Touch
Toxic Seriousness/Health/Schedules
Toxic Seeds of Unforgiveness

You **can choose** to change, choose to live in love or in fear. In the toxic soil watered by fear, you will struggle with your gift; in the soil of love, your gift will grow and mature.

We are not meant to be bound by chains. We have been given freedom in the Lord. We have the opportunity to overcome circumstances, including gift-blockers preventing us from living out the gifts we have been given.

> *You will keep in perfect peace all who trust in you, all whose thoughts are fixed on you!* (Isaiah 26:3 NLT).

CHAPTER 17
TOXIC THOUGHTS AS GIFT-BLOCKERS

Thoughts grow and change and influence every decision, word, action and physical reaction we make. If thoughts become toxic, they can become physically, emotionally or spiritually dangerous. Toxic thoughts trigger negative and anxious emotions, which produce biochemicals that stress the body.

Thoughts are real: They look like a tree with branches, and as they grow and become permanent, more branches grow and the connections become stronger.

Here are some toxic thoughts which activate discomfort levels:

- I can't do this.
- I am so stressed.
- I can't cope.
- I know it won't work.
- I hate school.
- I hate my job.
- I am not artistic.
- I don't have the energy to make a change.
- Nothing ever seems to go right for me.
- I will start my diet tomorrow.
- If only I were smarter.
- Mondays are not good days for me.

Toxic thinking will likely produce some kind of fruit or combination of fruit – addictions, anxieties, learning problems, physical illness, depression – because of the mind-body link. Toxic thoughts happen when we operate **out of our gift.**

We break the toxic gift-blockers by:

1. Choosing to capture those thoughts by using the powerful frontal lobe God has given us to stand outside of ourselves evaluating our thoughts and applying Godly wisdom to manage them.

CHAPTER 17 Toxic Thoughts as Gift-Blockers

PAGE 101

2. Identifying discomfort zones to help recognize toxic thoughts that are gift-blockers.
3. Rewiring which starts with repentance and forgiveness.
4. Choosing to operate in love, in the promises of the Lord.

Questions:

Name some of the toxic thoughts that are gift-blockers:

1. _____
2. _____
3. _____
4. _____
5. _____
6. _____

If you have experienced toxic thoughts, what were they and how did they make you feel?

_____
_____
_____

What can toxic thoughts do to your body?

_____
_____
_____

Name four ways we break the toxic gift-blockers.

1. _____
2. _____
3. _____

4. _____

Do you operate in fear or in love on a consistent basis? Explain:

_____
_____
_____

Memory Verse

Finally, brothers, whatever is true, whatever is noble, whatever is right, whatever is pure, whatever is lovely, whatever is admirable – if anything is excellent or praiseworthy – think about such things (Philippians 4:8 NIV).

Write down what this verse means to you.

_____
_____
_____

NOTES

_____
_____
_____
_____
_____
_____
_____
_____

CHAPTER 17 Toxic Thoughts as Gift-Blockers

NOTES

> We use God's mighty weapons, not worldly weapons, to knock down the strongholds of human reasoning and to destroy false arguments (2 Corinthians 10:4 NLT).

CHAPTER 18
TOXIC EMOTIONS AS GIFT-BLOCKERS

Toxic emotions and toxic thoughts are inseparable. That's because our thoughts have an emotional component attached to them.

When you think, you will also feel because thoughts build with the chemicals of emotion.

All emotions stem from love or fear, fear being the abnormal emotions. If negative feelings dominate, a neurochemical rush can start to distort feelings in the direction of fear, which can result in stress. This will affect your ability to think with clarity and will block your gift.

We break the gift-blocker of toxic emotions by:

1. Using the balancing circuit between the frontal lobe and the amygdala to balance reason and emotion.
2. Using the discomfort zones to help identify these gift-blocking emotions.
3. Capturing our thoughts.
4. Never doing this without prayer and the help of the Holy Spirit.
5. Rewiring, which begins with repentance and forgiveness.

To truly live out who God created you to be, you need to recognize your authority over gift-blockers. You can choose to walk in confidence that your gift is intentional and has a purpose.

Questions:

Why are toxic emotions and toxic thoughts inseparable?

_____

_____

CHAPTER 18 Toxic Emotions as Gift-Blockers

What emotions get in the way of your potential emotional and spiritual growth?
___
___
___

Do you know what has caused these toxic emotions to develop?
___
___
___

List ways that we can break the gift-blockers of toxic emotions:

1. ___
2. ___
3. ___
4. ___

Are you walking in the confidence that your gift is intentional and purposeful? How? If you are not, why not?
___
___
___

Memory Verse

Long ago the Lord said to Israel: "I have loved you, my people, with an everlasting love. With unfailing love I have drawn you to myself" (Jeremiah 31:3 NLT).

Write down what this verse means to you.
___

NOTES

CHAPTER 18 Toxic Emotions as Gift-Blockers

NOTES

> Words kill, words give life; they're either poison or fruit – you choose (Proverbs 18:21 *The Message*).

CHAPTER 19
TOXIC WORDS AS GIFT-BLOCKERS

The words we say can have a drastic impact on others – because they are an actual stream of electrical impulses – just as others' words can have a drastic impact on us. When unkind or misunderstood words hurt us, studies show that the same area of the brain (the cingulate gyrus) is impacted as when you are injured physically. The pain is the same, if not greater.

Words spoken over us can become toxic and turn into gift-blockers and have potential to have devastating effects on our lives. Being compared to others, hearing someone talk bad about you, misunderstanding something a parent tells you, all have gift-blocking potential.

One way to overcome the effects of toxic words is, surprisingly, also with words – loving words. Words spoken in love help heal and rewire the toxic thoughts caused by toxic words. We can choose not to take to heart the toxic words spoken over us, and forgiving those who have hurt us further strengthens love's power over toxic words.

Questions:

What happens to the brain when unkind words hurt us?

_____
_____
_____

What toxic words have hurt you?

_____
_____

CHAPTER 19 Toxic Words as Gift-Blockers

Who spoke these words over you?
_____
_____
_____

Did you take this person's words to heart or did you refuse to accept them?
_____
_____
_____

How did you react to them?
_____
_____
_____

Have you forgiven those who have hurt you?
_____
_____
_____

Have you spoken words that have hurt others?
_____
_____
_____

Have you asked them to forgive you?
_____
_____

Have you encouraged others with your spoken or written words?

_____
_____
_____

Memory Verse

Kind words are like honey – sweet to the soul and healthy for the body (Proverbs 16:24 NLT).

Write down what this verse means to you.

_____
_____
_____
_____
_____
_____
_____
_____
_____
_____
_____
_____
_____

CHAPTER 19 Toxic Words as Gift-Blockers

NOTES

> . . . *let us continue to love one another, for love comes from God. Anyone who loves is a child of God and knows God* (1 John 4:7 NLT).

CHAPTER 20
TOXIC LOVE AS A GIFT-BLOCKER

Love in its original and intended state is life-giving – however, love misunderstood and misused can be toxic. True love is never based upon appearances only. You must love someone for who they truly are, their likes and dislikes, their quirks and talents, their good and bad habits. To do otherwise can be toxic.

We base our relationships on our background, what we've gone through. No two people will have the same life outlook because no two people have the same background. The plasticity of the brain is what allows us each to develop our own unique outlook and have our own unique responses to different situations.

Because we are all so very different from one another, we can only love someone truly when we love them despite all their differences, despite the things they do that may annoy us. When we love this way, when we reach out to people in kindness and to help them, we are experiencing healthy love, and healthy love increases health, intelligence and happiness. It also rewires the brain and helps erase past memories and the heartache of toxic love.

Questions:

On what do you base your relationships?

_____

_____

_____

Do you love others unconditionally? What does unconditional love mean to you?

_____

_____

CHAPTER 20 Toxic Love as a Gift-Blocker

What has someone done that has hurt you? If you had understood each other's differences better, could this hurt have been avoided?

_____
_____
_____

Have you reached out to this person since he or she hurt you?

_____
_____
_____

Have you forgiven him or her? Have you forgiven yourself? Have you forgiven God?

_____
_____
_____

How have you acted in love toward him or her?

_____
_____
_____

Is there someone whom you have hurt that you need to reach out to and ask for forgiveness and take steps to mend the friendship?

_____
_____
_____
_____

Memory Verse

But anyone who does not love does not know God, for God is love (1 John 4:8 NLT).

Write down what this verse means to you.

_____
_____
_____
_____
_____
_____
_____
_____

NOTES

_____
_____
_____
_____
_____
_____
_____
_____

CHAPTER 20 Toxic Love as a Gift-Blocker

PAGE 115

NOTES

> *The Lord is with me; I will not be afraid* (Psalm 118:6 NIV).

CHAPTER 21
TOXIC DREAMS AS GIFT-BLOCKERS

Dreams occur during REM (rapid eye movement) sleep. As you REM sleep, your brain sorts out toxic and nontoxic thoughts through your dreams. Toxic thought clusters disturb the nerve chemistry and electrical-chemical feedback loops of the brain and body, causing you to forget your dreams.

The dream process starts with NREM (non-rapid eye movement) sleep where the brain stops processing the outside world and progresses into REM sleep. There we process our inner thought life. Since dreams involve abstract ideas, they can be confusing.

While awake, serotonin and norepinephrine help us think logically, giving us a burst of acetylcholine when something captures our attention. While asleep, acetylcholine is active, consolidating our memories, while serotonin and norepinephrine shut down. Acetylcholine brings the "strangeness" to our dreams.

Since dreams sort our thinking, a recurring dream may indicate a toxic thought that needs to be resolved. I had a recurring dream that someone was breaking into my childhood home, which did happen when I was very young. It was the same root of fear but three different scenarios. As an adult, I still get traumatized when I recall the dreams. They're less frequent now, but when I do dream about it, I know I need to rewire that fear circuit.

We can break the gift-blocker of toxic dreams by:

1. Observing and journaling your dreams to increase awareness.
2. Prayerfully asking the Holy Spirit to tell you what the dreams mean.

Questions:

Do you remember your dreams? If so, how much detail do you usually remember?

_____

CHAPTER 21 Toxic Dreams as Gift-Blockers

_____
_____
_____

Have you experienced toxic dreams, dreams you found confusing, disturbing, or frightening? How did the dreams make you feel?

_____
_____
_____

Have your dreams ever influenced your decision about an important issue in your life? How?

_____
_____
_____

What two things can you do to break the gift-blocker of toxic dreams:

1. _____
2. _____

Memory Verse

I will put my trust in Him (Isaiah 8:17 NIV).

Write down what this verse means to you.

_____
_____
_____
_____

NOTES

CHAPTER 21 Toxic Dreams as Gift-Blockers

NOTES

> For wisdom will enter your heart, and knowledge will be pleasant to your soul (Proverbs 2:10 NIV).

CHAPTER 22
TOXIC CHOICES AS GIFT-BLOCKERS

In one day, we make all kinds of choices from the mundane – what to eat, what to wear – to the serious – what to do about our lives or how to deal with a problem. Choices we make are determined by our thoughts. The healthier and more submitted our thoughts are to Christ, the healthier our choices will be. The more toxic our thoughts and attitudes, the more toxic the choices we make.

When you walk in the structure of the gift God has given you, according to His will for your life, you will make healthy choices, which can overcome regret, doubt and unforgiveness caused by toxic choices.

I had to make a choice, one of the hardest in my life, whether to stay married. My husband, Mac, was drinking due to toxic seeds from his childhood. I knew I had to trust God so I wrote Mac a letter explaining that I was letting go and giving him to God. My husband made the healthy choice to sell out to Christ. He's now a model husband and father.

God is forgiving and has blessed you with a brain, modeled after His own, a brain you can rewire (neuroplasticity) to help you make the right choices. But you have to take the first step to change your thinking and your choices.

We break the gift-blocker of toxic choices by:

1. Using the discomfort zones to help identify and acknowledge gift-blocking caused by toxic thoughts.

2. Using the frontal lobe to stand outside of ourselves and observe our own thinking and choices and realize their consequences.

3. Rewiring the thought networks, starting with repentance and forgiveness.

4. Never doing this without prayer and the help of the Holy Spirit.

CHAPTER 22 Toxic Choices as Gift-Blockers

Questions:

Choices we make are determined by what?

_____
_____
_____

I shared a personal story about the choice I made about my marriage. Have you ever faced a personal dilemma where you had to make a choice? What was it and how did you come to your decision?

_____
_____
_____

Have you ever made a toxic choice that has had a lasting impact on your life?

_____
_____
_____

We break the gift-blockers of toxic choices by:

1. _____
2. _____
3. _____
4. _____

Memory Verse

For the Lord gives wisdom, and from his mouth come knowledge and understanding (Proverbs 2:6 NIV).

Write down what this verse means to you.

NOTES

CHAPTER 22 Toxic Choices as Gift-Blockers

PAGE 123

NOTES

> *The Lord is compassionate and gracious . . .* (Psalm 103:8 NIV).

CHAPTER 23
TOXIC TOUCH AS A GIFT-BLOCKER

Touch is described as "one of the most essential elements of human development" and a "powerful healing force." Two thousand years ago, Jesus touched those He healed.

Yet toxic touch can turn what should be a healing and healthy human connection into an ugly gift-blocker. When touch becomes toxic, toxic seeds and emotions and thoughts become part of the reaction. However, another aspect of toxic touch is the lack of touch.

Animal and human studies have demonstrated the benefits of touch. Scientists found that baby rhesus monkeys experienced stress, trauma and depression when they were deprived of their mothers' touch. When touch is withheld, missing, exaggerated, muted or otherwise distorted, perceptions and responses become toxic thoughts. Affectionate touch is an essential "nutrient" to normal brain functioning.

Neurons in the top and side of the brain get excited and start firing in the brain of the person receiving the hug. A mirror neuron firing also happens in the person who decides to reach out and hug someone.

We must break the gift-blocker of toxic touch by:

1. Using our discomfort zones to help identify and acknowledge gift-blocking toxic touch . . . is it appropriate or lacking?
2. Using the frontal lobe to stand outside of ourselves and evaluate how this can be changed.
3. Rewiring, starting with repentance and forgiveness.
4. Never doing this without prayer and the help of the Holy Spirit.

Healthy touch is one of the physical things you can do to change your mental processes and unblock your gift.

CHAPTER 23 Toxic Touch as a Gift-Blocker

Questions:

Inappropriate touch is a gift-blocker. What is another aspect of toxic touch?

_____
_____
_____

What can you do to break the gift-blocker of toxic touch?

_____
_____
_____

Have you ever experienced toxic touch, and how did it make you feel?

_____
_____
_____

Are you a demonstrative person, hugging others? Why or why not?

_____
_____
_____

Memory Verse

For great is his love toward us, and the faithfulness of the Lord endures forever (Psalm 117:2 NIV).

Write down what this verse means to you.

_____
_____

NOTES

CHAPTER 23 Toxic Touch as a Gift-Blocker

NOTES

> *Laughter is the best medicine* (see Proverbs 17:22).

CHAPTER 24
TOXIC SERIOUSNESS AS A GIFT-BLOCKER

Toxic seriousness, schedules and health all work hand-in-hand to block our gifts. Jesus came to give us life more abundantly, but when we are toxic and not walking in our gift, this pours out into our outlook and our schedules. We can get too serious.

Having fun will detox your gift-blockers, improve health, relieve stress and make you smart. Laughter releases an instant flood of feel-good chemicals, boosting the immune system. A good laugh can make cortisol drop by 39%, adrenalin by 70% and increase the "feel-good" hormone endorphin by 29%. Humor gets both sides of your brain working together and increases your energy level.

While having fun and laughing, throw in an exercise routine to boost your gift. Exercise makes the heart pump faster and more efficiently. Increased blood flow nourishes and cleans the brain and other organs. If you break into a sweat, you also get the added benefit of mood improvement with the release of endorphins.

Using your time wisely and exercising regularly are important for clear thinking.

Questions:

What does laughter physically do to our bodies?

_____
_____
_____
_____

CHAPTER 24 Toxic Seriousness as a Gift-Blocker

Name three things that having fun will do for you?

_____
_____
_____

Do you laugh regularly? How do you feel after you've had a good laugh?

_____
_____
_____

What do you do for fun?

_____
_____
_____

What can you do to incorporate more fun into your life?

_____
_____
_____

If you are tired and stressed all the time, what are some things you could cut out or do to release the stress and bring energy?

_____
_____
_____

List some things you've always wanted to do for fun and start trying to do them.

_____

Do you have an exercise program? If so, how often? If not, do you plan to start one?

Memory Verse

There is a time for everything, and a season for every activity under heaven . . . a time to laugh . . . and a time to dance (Ecclesiastes 3:1,4 NIV).

Write down what these verses mean to you.

CHAPTER 24 Toxic Seriousness as a Gift-Blocker

NOTES

> *Bear with each other and forgive whatever grievances you may have against one another. Forgive as the Lord forgave you (Colossians 3:13 NIV).*

CHAPTER 25
TOXIC SEEDS OF UNFORGIVENESS AS GIFT-BLOCKERS

All gift-blockers grow from a tiny seed and are watered with the attention we give them. When we don't forgive, hanging on to pain and events, we are growing toxic seeds.

Each time something is brought into consciousness, it will change, getting worse or better – this is up to you. Sometimes people say "I can't," but "I can't" is also a decision.

It's difficult to let go of unjust things that happened to you, but they will get worse when you give them more attention. The world's approach is to indulge, speak about, tear apart and wallow; yet this does not bring about healing. We need to acknowledge and repent for hanging on to unforgiveness, and then we need to deliberately forgive. Forgiveness places the situation in God's hands. Squashing the toxic thoughts is not the answer because they are still alive in your nonconscious mind, occupying mental real estate and affecting your spirit, soul and body.

You cannot control the event but you can control your reaction to the event. Repentance and forgiveness stop worry and anxiety and acknowledge God's sovereignty, putting Him back on the throne to do what He is supposed to do.

Read Romans 7:15-25 about the apostle Paul's struggle with the cycle of sin, repentance and forgiveness.

When we forgive, we rewire, and as we plant new seed and walk in confidence, amazing change can happen.

CHAPTER 25 Toxic Seeds of Unforgiveness as Gift-Blockers

Questions:

Have you found it difficult to forgive?

_____
_____
_____

Are you squashing toxic thoughts hoping if you don't think about them, they will go away? Do a real, honest soul search and examine how you feel physically and mentally as these thoughts move into your conscious mind.

_____
_____
_____

Do you know why you're having difficulty forgiving this person?

_____
_____
_____

Examine your life. Can you see where unforgiveness has actually hurt you? Look deeply.

_____
_____
_____

What steps could you take to move in forgiveness toward this person?

_____
_____
_____

Think of a time you hurt someone, did he or she forgive you? Did you ask for forgiveness?

_____
_____
_____

How do you believe walking in forgiveness could change your life right now?

_____
_____
_____

What changes could you make to live your life ready to forgive?

_____
_____
_____

Memory Verse

For if you forgive men when they sin against you, your heavenly Father will also forgive you. But if you do not forgive men their sins, your Father will not forgive your sins (Matthew 6:14-15 NIV).

Write down what these verses mean to you.

_____
_____
_____
_____

CHAPTER 25 Toxic Seeds of Unforgiveness as Gift-Blockers

NOTES

Conclusion

For we are God's masterpiece. He has created us anew in Christ Jesus, so we can do the good things he planned for us long ago (Ephesians 2:10 NLT).

Our minds, thought processes and abilities to choose are fashioned after God. We think all day long and sort out our thoughts throughout the night. The unique way each of us "thinks to build thoughts" is the creational gift God has given us. Each of us is a masterpiece. This gift of unique "thinking" empowers you to control the very thing in control of who you are: your thought life. Proverbs 23:7 tells us that a man is what he thinks in his heart.

May you take this gift – your piece of eternity, your unique and special way of thinking – and use it to complete your divine purpose with deliberate and contagious energy, passion and excitement.

Once you discover the structure of your gift (how you think), think deeply to increase your intelligence and wisdom and go to the edges of your ability.

May you use the knowledge of how to identify "gift-blockers" not as a setback but as a step forward to rewiring and renewing the mind.

Take the next step into your gift! There is something you can do that no one else can!

Visit www.drleaf.net/detox to download a special guide to help you break free from toxic thinking.

Every good gift and every perfect gift is from above, and comes down from the Father of lights . . . (James 1:17).

NOTES

CHAPTER 25 Toxic Seeds of Unforgiveness as Gift-Blockers

NOTES

NOTES

CHAPTER 25 Toxic Seeds of Unforgiveness as Gift-Blockers

NOTES

NOTES

CHAPTER 25 Toxic Seeds of Unforgiveness as Gift-Blockers

NOTES